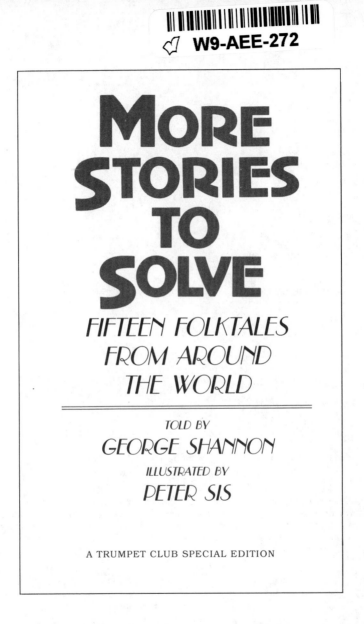

MORE STORIES TO SOLVE

FIFTEEN FOLKTALES FROM AROUND THE WORLD

TOLD BY
GEORGE SHANNON

ILLUSTRATED BY
PETER SIS

A TRUMPET CLUB SPECIAL EDITION

Published by The Trumpet Club
666 Fifth Avenue, New York, New York 10103

Text copyright © 1989, 1990 by George W.B. Shannon
Illustrations copyright © 1990 by Peter Sis

ISBN 0-440-84674-9

This edition published by arrangement with Greenwillow Books,
a division of William Morrow & Company, Inc.
Printed in the United States of America
April 1992

CWO   10 9 8 7 6 5 4 3 2 1

*TO ALL WHO SMILED
AND ASKED FOR MORE*

CONTENTS

INTRODUCTION

Stories and mysteries have existed for as long as there have been people to tell them. And for just as long, there have been heroes who succeed through their ability to solve puzzles. These characters, who often have no rights, no power, no money, and no physical strength, are able to solve their dilemmas by finding fresh ways of looking at a situation. If they cannot see the solutions themselves, they are wise enough to accept advice from those who can. Like these quiet heroes, the reader can solve the following stories by careful listening or reading and by exploring different approaches to finding the answers.

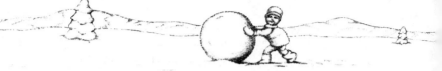

1.

THE SNOWMAN

*O*nce, when it began to snow, three brothers decided they would make the biggest snowman their village had ever seen. All three rolled their snowballs bigger and bigger, and bigger still. When each ball got too big for one to push, two pushed, then all three together. When they couldn't move the biggest of the three balls anymore, they stopped.

The brothers tried to lift and stack the second ball on top of the first, but they could not. They had done such a good job of making them big that they were too heavy to lift. They were beginning to scrape the snowballs down to make them smaller when their grandfather came home.

"Aren't you doing that backward?" he asked.

When they explained their problem, their grandfather said, "You don't need less. You need more." And he told them what to do.

By the time their supper was ready, the boys had finished making the biggest snowman their village had ever seen. It was as tall as all three boys sitting on one another's shoulders. How could they have done this?

HOW IT WAS DONE

The "more" their grandfather told them
about was to pack a ramp of snow against
the biggest ball of snow. Their second
snowball was too heavy to lift, but not too
heavy to roll uphill. After building the snow
ramp higher and rolling up the third
snowball, they simply dug away the ramp
and left their snowman standing.

2.

THE NEW PRINCE

King Leopard needed an heir to take his place when he died, but he had no sons. It was decided that a contest would be held and the winner would become prince.

"This spear will be the test," announced King Leopard. "Whoever can throw it up in the air while dancing and count to ten before catching it will be named my son and prince."

Of course, all the animals were eager to try. It seemed an easy test. Elephant insisted on being first. His dance was clumsy, and he had counted only to four when the spear fell to the ground. Ox was next. His dance was somewhat better, and he threw the spear a little higher; but it still hit the ground before he'd counted to five. Ape was next, and others followed. None of them could count to ten before the spear hit the ground beside them.

When the little deer said he wanted to try, everyone laughed.

"Rules are rules," said the king. "Everyone here may have his chance."

The little deer picked up the spear and danced a lovely light-footed dance. As he danced, he threw up the spear and easily counted to ten before catching it again. That very day he was crowned prince. How did the little deer succeed when the larger, stronger animals had failed?

HOW IT WAS DONE

He counted to ten by fives (five, ten).
The king hadn't said *how* they were to count to ten.

3.

ALL FOR
ONE COIN

*T*here once lived a wealthy merchant in Kashmir whose son was as lazy as he was foolish. No matter what the merchant said his son did the opposite. If, that is, he did anything at all. The merchant finally had all he could take.

"I want you to go to the marketplace," he told his son, "and buy something for us to eat, something for us to drink, something for the cow to eat, and something for us to plant in the garden. *And* you may spend only this one small coin. If you can do it, come back home. If you can't, don't come home."

As the boy walked toward the marketplace, he began to cry. He could not think of any way to buy all those things with the coin his father had given him. He'd never be able to go home. He was crying so loudly a girl working in the field heard him and asked what was wrong. When he told her about his father's orders and all he had to buy with one small coin, the girl shook her head and told him not to worry. She said he could easily do what his father wanted and told him how.

That night the boy went home with a smile on his face as well as something to eat, something to drink, something to feed the cow, and something to plant in the garden. His father was very surprised *and* very impressed. How did the boy do it?

HOW IT WAS DONE

He bought a watermelon: its flesh to eat, its juice to drink, the rind for the cow to eat, and its seeds to plant in the garden.

4.

FIREFLY
AND THE
APES

One night in the jungle Firefly was flashing
his light and flying circles around Ape's head.

"Go home!" yelled Ape, and laughed. "You
shouldn't be out at night if you're afraid of the
dark."

Firefly said he wasn't, but Ape argued back.

"You're so afraid of the dark you always have
to have a light with you."

Firefly tried to explain that every firefly has a
flashing light, but Ape said that just meant that
all fireflies were afraid of the dark.

"I'll prove I'm not afraid of anything," said Firefly. "Come to my house tomorrow night, and we'll have a contest—a fight!"

The idea of a contest with tiny Firefly made Ape laugh even louder.

"I can squash you with two fingers. You'd better bring all your friends and relatives because you're going to need all the help you can get."

"Maybe you're the one who'd better bring friends," challenged Firefly. "That is, if you're not afraid to come."

News of the contest quickly spread. The next evening everyone was waiting by Firefly's house.

When Ape arrived, he smiled and said, "I'm all ready to squash you flat." He had a big wooden club over his shoulder. "And I did what you said. I brought a few friends in case I need help fighting little you!"

When Ape motioned, ninety-nine more apes came down the path, and each one carried a big wooden club. Now it was one hundred apes with one hundred clubs against one little firefly. A bird called, "One . . . two . . . three . . . start!" and all one hundred apes raised their clubs and began to walk toward Firefly.

The fight was fast and furious, but by the end of the evening every one of the apes was lying on the ground and Firefly was the winner. How could this have happened?

HOW IT WAS DONE

Firefly simply flew from one ape's nose to the next, and when the apes tried to hit him, they kept hitting each other instead.

5.

THE FROG

Once long ago on a summer day, a frog out looking for adventure found a wooden bucket filled with fresh cream. He smiled to himself, then jumped right in! It felt wonderful, all cool and silky against his skin. He played and splashed and swam to the left and then to the right.

After a while he was ready to go home and tell everyone about what he'd done. He was ready to go, but he couldn't get out. The bucket was too deep for him to touch the bottom and push out

through the cream. There were no rocks or logs like the ones in his pond. And the sides of the bucket were too slippery to climb. He was trapped. His only choice was to keep swimming or drown.

The frog couldn't bear the thought of drowning, especially in cream. He swam to the left and then to the right, around and around till his arms and legs were too tired to move.

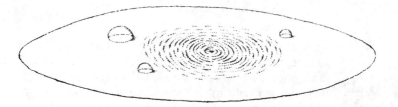

It's no use, he told himself. The end is the end. I might as well get it over with.

He swam to the center of the bucket and began to sink. But as soon as the cream covered his mouth, he sputtered out, "*No*," and started swimming again.

After a while his arms and legs again grew too tired to move. Again he swam to the center and began to sink. And once again, when the cream began to cover his face, he sputtered out, *"No,"* and started swimming.

But the fifth time this happened he sank only a little bit before he felt something beneath his feet. It was soft and slippery, but still solid enough to hold him.

The frog pushed down and hopped out of the bucket and back to his friends as fast as he could go. When he told them what happened, they all wanted to know how he finally got out. But the frog didn't know. Do you know how?

HOW IT WAS DONE

All his swimming around had begun to churn the cream into fresh soft butter.

6.

THE LAWYER AND THE DEVIL

*O*nce there was a man in Ireland who said he would do anything to get money to send his three sons to school. When the devil heard this, he proposed a trade. The devil would pay for the boys' education in exchange for their father's soul.

Seven years later the devil returned to claim the boys' father.

Neither the father himself nor his sons wanted him to die. The eldest son, who had in the meantime become a priest, begged the devil to let their father live just a few more years. Finally the devil agreed. The next time the devil came, the second son, who had become a doctor, also begged the devil to let their father live just a few years longer. Finally the devil agreed again. When the devil came a third time, it was the third son, who had become a lawyer, who pleaded with him.

"I know you've already delayed taking our father two times, and you can't be expected to do it again," he said to the devil. "But please, could you just let him live as long as that little stub of a candle on the table lasts? Surely you'll grant us time to say good-bye."

The devil looked at the little stub of a candle burning on the table and agreed. The old man didn't have to die that day and was assured that the devil could never take his soul. Why?

HOW IT WAS DONE

The lawyer walked over and blew out
the candle, making sure it would last
forever. He had said "as long as that
little stub of a candle lasts," not "as long
as the candle burns."

7.

CROWING KETTLES

Once years ago a traveling preacher stopped for the night at an inn in the country. Not long after the preacher had fallen asleep, other folks came to the inn to gamble and drink. Before long, some money was missing, and they all were arguing at the top of their lungs. When the preacher heard the ruckus, he got up to see what the trouble was.

He told them if they'd just quiet down and give him a little help, he'd be able to solve everything.

He had them get a rooster and a big old kettle from the fireplace. After he had covered the rooster with the kettle and covered the fireplace as well, he blew out all the candles and lamps.

"Covered roosters always catch a thief," said the preacher. "I want everyone to come up and touch this kettle. When the thief puts a finger on it, the rooster will crow and I'll grab him right then and there."

Everyone there shuffled up through the dark to touch the kettle, but the rooster never crowed.

"Sorry," said the preacher. "Must be a sickly rooster. Light the lamps and candles, and stir up the fire."

By the time people could see in the room again, the preacher knew who had taken the money. How?

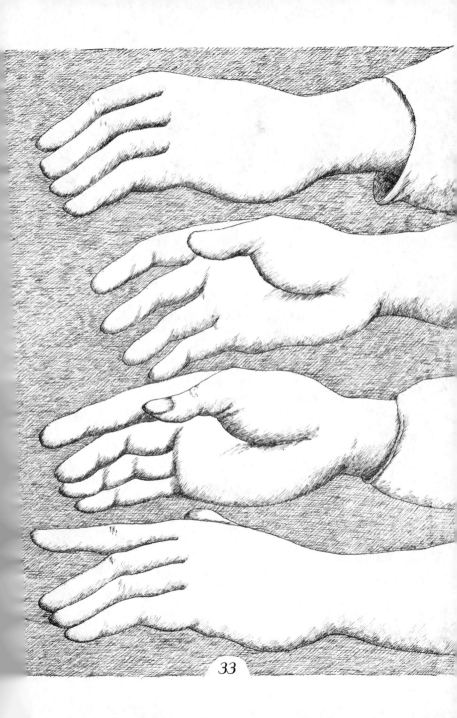

HOW IT WAS DONE

Worried that the rooster might really crow,
the thief had not touched the old kettle. His
hands were the only ones without any soot
from its bottom.

8.

NEVER SEEN, NEVER HEARD

*I*n ancient times many kings competed with riddles instead of fighting wars. After solving the riddle the Egyptian king Nactanabo had sent him, King Lycurgus of Babylon wanted to send him a challenge in return. To make sure everything would go in his favor, King Lycurgus sent the cleverest man he knew, Aesop, storyteller and former slave.

Aesop quickly outwitted King Nactanabo, but the king would not let Aesop leave. King Nactanabo hoped to disgrace Aesop and send him home in defeat rather than with a tribute to his king. He tested Aesop with riddle after riddle, but Aesop easily solved each one. Finally King Nactanabo came up with an impossible task for Aesop.

"If you can bring me something that I've never seen or heard about," the king told Aesop, "I'll send one thousand dollars as a tribute to your king. If you fail, you must leave and admit both your and your king's defeat."

Aesop begged to have three days to find something so rare that the king would never have seen it or even heard of it. King Nactanabo agreed. He knew that no matter what Aesop brought or told him, all he had to do was say he'd already seen it. His advisers were ordered to say the same thing.

When Aesop returned, he handed King Nactanabo a small piece of paper. Just as planned, the king and his advisers all said, "We've seen this before. We know all about it. You have failed."

"That's good," said Aesop. "Now I'll take the one thousand dollars for my king."

"No!" said King Nactanabo. "I've never seen this paper before."

"Good," said Aesop. "I've passed your test and will accept the one-thousand-dollar tribute for my king."

There was nothing King Nactanabo or his advisers could do or say. If the king said he *had* seen the paper, he had to pay King Lycurgus one thousand dollars. And if he said he *had not* seen the paper, he had to pay King Lycurgus one thousand dollars. What words had Aesop written on the paper?

HOW IT WAS DONE

*"I, King Nactanabo,
owe King Lycurgus
one thousand dollars
to be paid to Aesop."*
(SIGNED)
"King Nactanabo"

38

9.

THE BRAHMAN AND THE BANKER

A Brahman and his wife once decided to go on a religious pilgrimage. To make certain that the small amount of money they had—seven hundred rupees—remained safe, they asked a banker friend to keep it for them. Because the banker declined several times before agreeing to keep it, the Brahman thought it would be an insult to ask him for a receipt.

Their trip went well. But when they got back home and went to get their money, the banker said they had never given him any to keep. Day after day the Brahman asked the banker for his money, and day after day the banker denied ever having received the Brahman's seven hundred rupees.

One day, while the Brahman was walking home from the banker's, a wealthy merchant's wife heard him crying. When she learned his problem, she quickly thought of a plan to get his money back. She told the Brahman to return to the banker's the next day at a specific time and ask for his money again. She said that she would be there, too, but that he must pretend not to know her.

The following day the woman went to the banker's a few minutes before the Brahman was to arrive. She told the banker she would like him to keep her many jewels while she was away. She was going to search for her husband, who was several weeks late coming home from a business trip. This time, when the Brahman came and asked for his money, the banker quickly gave it to him. A few moments later the woman's maid came to announce that the woman's husband had just returned. Since she no longer needed to travel, the woman kept her jewels and the Brahman went home with his money. How did the woman's plan suddenly make the banker change his ways?

HOW IT WAS DONE

Eager to get his hands on the
woman's jewels, the banker didn't
want to frighten her away by
appearing to have cheated a
Brahman out of such a small sum
of money.

10.

A LAST REQUEST

*I*n Chile there once lived a young ruler who thought cleverness was the most important thing of all. He was forever outwitting his advisers and often played jokes on others by asking them riddles that were impossibly difficult to answer. When it came time for him to marry, the young man said he would not marry anyone who was not as clever as he was. And so, everywhere he went, the young ruler asked the same riddle: "If you care for a basil plant tenderly, how many leaves will it grow?"

In village after village the young women ran away, embarrassed at not knowing the answer. That is, until he asked Carmelita. She looked into his eyes and said, "I will tell you, but only after you tell me how many fish now swim in the sea."

This time it was the young ruler who had no answer and left embarrassed. But he was also impressed. The next week, when Carmelita outwitted him again, he decided she was clever enough to be his wife. Carmelita agreed to marry him, but only on the condition that he grant her one last request when it came her time to die. He agreed, and her request was written on paper, signed, and sealed.

Carmelita was soon loved by everyone in the country. She helped the people solve their problems, and when her husband made an unjust decision, she told them how to make him change his mind. Usually the young ruler was proud of her cleverness, but one day, when she proved him wrong, he became furious.

"How dare you make everyone laugh at me! Your punishment is death."

Carmelita didn't argue, but she reminded him of his promise to grant her last request. It was only one sentence long, but it assured Carmelita that her husband would pardon her. In fact, he laughed and hugged her in appreciation of her cleverness. What was Carmelita's last request?

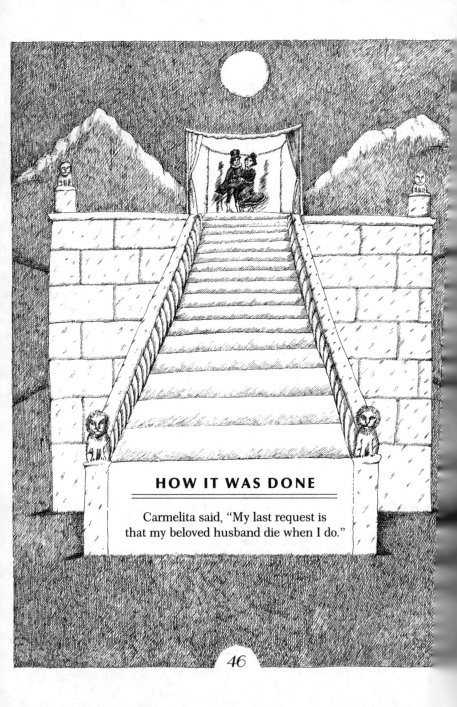

HOW IT WAS DONE

Carmelita said, "My last request is
that my beloved husband die when I do."

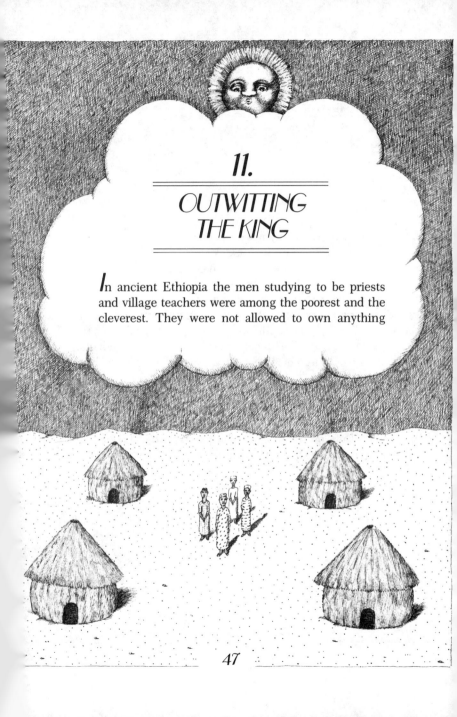

11.
OUTWITTING THE KING

*I*n ancient Ethiopia the men studying to be priests and village teachers were among the poorest and the cleverest. They were not allowed to own anything

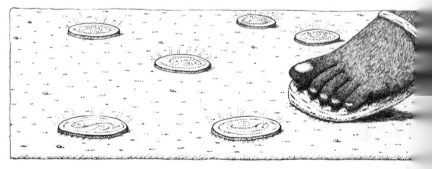

and so lived by their wits as they traveled around the country to study with monks.

Once a king decided he would catch not only every thief in his country but every potential thief as well. Knowing that the men studying to be village teachers were always in need of money, the king called them all to the palace. His plan was to scatter gold coins in the courtyard. The next morning, when the students passed through, he would arrest anyone who picked up a coin. The coins were scattered, and the students passed through the courtyard. No one bent down to pick up a coin, yet all the coins were gone when the students left.

Determined to catch the one who had taken the coins, the king invited all the students to a banquet

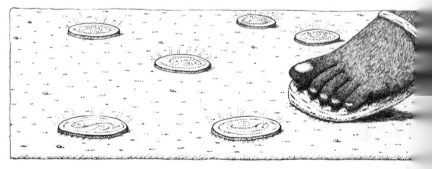

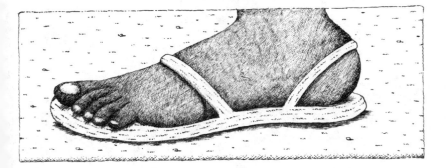

and to spend the night. There was lots of food and wine, and the king's spies were everywhere. If any of the spies heard a student bragging about stealing the coins, he was to make a secret mark on that student's arm while he slept. Then, when the students left the next morning, the king would look at their arms as they passed by and grab the thief himself.

One of the spies did hear a student boast how he'd picked up the gold coins by rubbing wax on the bottom of his shoes, and the spy made the secret mark on that student's arm. The next morning, as they all walked past, the king saw the secret mark, but he still could not figure out who had taken the coins. Why?

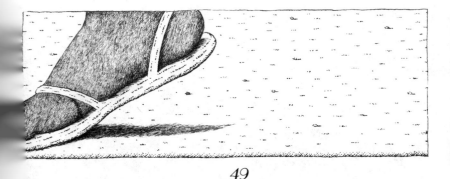

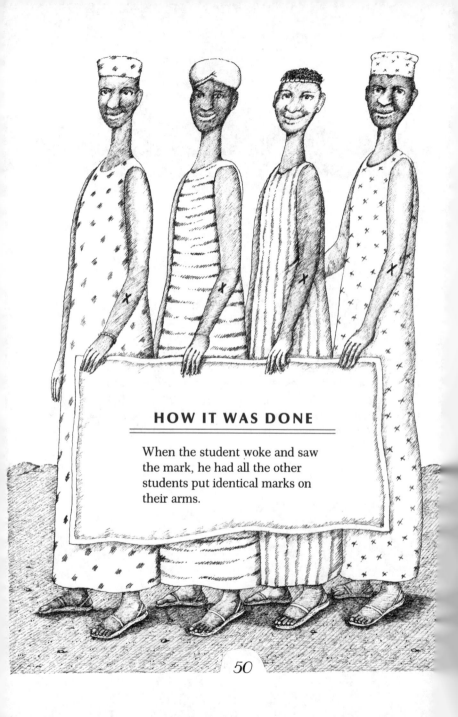

HOW IT WAS DONE

When the student woke and saw the mark, he had all the other students put identical marks on their arms.

12.

SUNRISE

One night long ago in Mexico, a frog and a deer had an argument. They decided to settle their differences with a bet.

"Twenty-five flies for the one who can see the first rays of the sun," said Frog.

Deer laughed and quickly agreed. "I will look to the east." He knew the sun always rises in the east. "You must look some other place."

Frog agreed. He quietly sat watching the highest mountain peak in the west while deer stared into the darkness of the eastern plain. After hours and hours of waiting and watching, Frog suddenly yelled, "Look! *I* see the first rays of the sun. I win."

When Deer turned to look west, he had to agree that Frog had been the first to see the rays of the sun *and* Frog had seen them by looking away from the sun.

How could this be?

HOW IT WAS DONE

Frog saw the sunlight reflecting off the peak of the mountain in the west while deer was watching the lower plain in the east. Mountains, being higher, always catch the sun's rays first as the earth turns to face the sun.

13.

THE TALLEST TALE

There once lived four men in Burma who loved to tell tall tales and impossible stories. One day a well-dressed stranger came to their village. They wanted his fine clothes and thought of a plan to get them. After visiting with him for a while, one of the men said, "Since we've all been travelers, why don't we each tell about our most wonderful adventure? But if anyone thinks a story isn't true, he must become the servant of the teller and do whatever he's ordered to do."

The traveler agreed, and the four men smiled. They were certain he wouldn't believe their impossible tales and thus be forced to become their servant.

The first man told how before he was born, he had climbed a tree too tall for his father to climb to pick some plums for his mother. The men waited for the traveler to say, "Impossible," but he only smiled in admiration.

The second man told how he'd gotten stuck in the top of a tree when he was only one week old and, when no one would help him, had gone to the village and gotten a ladder so he could climb down from the tree. Again the four men waited for the traveler to say, "Impossible," but he only nodded and smiled.

The traveler even believed the third man's story about catching a tiger and breaking it in two when he was only one year old, and the fourth man's tale of swimming for three days to the bottom of the sea, where he caught a mountain-size fish with his bare hands.

The four men were disappointed that the traveler believed them. Now they could not make him their servant and order him to give them his clothes. On the other hand, all they had to do was say they believed his story no matter how impossible it turned out to be, and they, too, would be safe.

"Your turn," they told the traveler. "Tell us your best adventure."

He did, and when he had finished, the four men had to give up their clothes despite the fact that they said they believed him. How did this happen?

HOW IT WAS DONE

The stranger told how he had once had four
servants who loved to tell stories and wear
fine clothes. The four servants had taken
his clothes and run away. He said that these
four men were those very same men and
that since their clothes were really his, they
had to give them back. If the four men
admitted his story was true, they had to give
him their clothes. If they said it wasn't, they
had to become his servants and do what he
ordered them to do. Whatever they said,
they had to give the stranger their clothes.

14.

THE BET

*I*n the old South when people claimed they could own other people, there lived a slave, named John, who could outsmart anybody for miles around. He was always making bets, and he never made a bet he didn't win. This only made people more eager to bet with him. Everyone, including Colonel Blake, wanted to say that he'd been the first to outsmart John.

"I'll bet you," John said to him one day, "that I can stand at one end of your parlor and throw a raw egg all the way across the room and onto the fireplace mantel without breaking the egg. I'll bet you fifty dollars, all the money I have."

The colonel quickly agreed to the bet. He was certain nobody could throw a raw egg without having it break.

"I'll even give you a dozen tries," he told John.

The first egg John threw smashed on the edge of the mantel. The second hit the candlestick sitting on top. The third egg smashed and smeared the painting above the mantel, but the colonel just laughed. He was happy because he was going to be able to say he was the first to outsmart John on a bet. John threw all twelve eggs, but not one landed without breaking.

"Looks as if I won the bet," said Colonel Blake with a bragging smile.

"Yes," said John. "Sure looks that way."

He paid him the fifty dollars, but when John went to bed that night, he still had fifty dollars from winning a bet. Where did it come from?

HOW IT WAS DONE

John had also made a bet for a hundred
dollars with the neighboring plantation
owner. He bet he could throw eggs all over
Colonel Blake's parlor and that the colonel
would only watch and laugh. By losing the
first bet on purpose, John had managed to
outsmart both men at the same time.

15.
THE SHIP

Theseus, a great hero of ancient Greece, had a ship he prized above all others. Whenever a board rotted or broke, he immediately had it replaced with a new one to make certain the ship would last forever. One by one the boards had to be replaced until every board in the ship was new.

But if all the boards in the ship are new, wondered Theseus, is the ship still the old one I wanted to keep? Or is it a completely new ship? And if so, when did it stop being my old ship and start being a new ship? None of his advisers could give him an answer. Can you?

HOW IT WAS DONE

No one yet has been able to find an answer.
Sometimes the wisest answer may be
that there is no answer.

NOTES

1. I first encountered the basic plot of THE SNOWMAN more than ten years ago in a thin, dilapidated book of Korean folktales. I have not been able to find that book again or any other version of the story. In the version I read so long ago the story took place on a beach with large stones rather than snow.

2. THE NEW PRINCE is a Liberian folktale retold from *African Wonder Tales,* edited by Frances Carpenter (Doubleday, 1963). It can also be found in *With a Deep Sea Smile,* edited by Virginia Tashjian (Little, Brown, 1974).

3. ALL FOR ONE COIN is a folktale from Kashmir retold from *Folk-Tales of Kashmir,* collected by J. Hinton Knowles (Kegan Paul, 1893).

4. FIREFLY AND THE APES is a Visayan folktale from the Philippines retold from "Arnomongo and Iput-Iput," collected by Berton L. Maxfield and W. H. Millington in *The Journal of American Folklore* 20 (1907): 314–315. Variants are told by peoples of the Western Pacific and Southeast Asia, including the Hmong, recent immigrants to the United States. A German variant can be found in *The Complete Grimm's Fairy Tales.*

5. THE FROG is a Russian folktale. It is retold from *The Lazies: Tales of the Peoples of Russia,* translated and edited by Mirra Ginsburg (Macmillan, 1973), and *Baba Yaga's Geese, and Other Russian Stories,* translated and adapted by Bonnie Carey (Indiana University Press, 1973). Carey worked from L. Panteleev, "Dve lyagushki," *Lukomor'e.*

6. Folktales in which someone may live as long as a candle burns exist throughout Europe. Antti Aarne refers to Flemish variants in *The Types of the Folktale* (Burt Franklin, 1971, reprint of 1928 edition). Katharine M. Briggs cites several variants in *A Dictionary of British Folk-Tales in the English Language* (Indiana University Press, 1971). W. B. Yeats included a literary variant in *Irish Fairy Tales* (1892). THE LAWYER AND THE DEVIL is retold from *Irish Folktales,* edited by Henry Glassie (Pantheon, 1985). Glassie worked from Michael J. Murphy's *Now You're Talking* (Belfast: Blackstaff Press, 1975).

7. CROWING KETTLES is a United States folktale retold from *American Folk Tales and Songs,* edited by Richard Chase (New American Library, 1965), who heard it from Smith Harmon in North Carolina. A New Jersey variant has been collected by Henry Charlton Beck in *New York Folklore Quarterly* 4 (1948): 48–49.

8. NEVER SEEN, NEVER HEARD is a folktale about Aesop retold from *Aesop Without Morals,* edited by Lloyd W. Daly (Thomas Yoseloff, 1961). A Russian variant can be found in *Eurasian Folk and Fairy Tales,* edited by I. F. Bulatkin (Criterion, 1965).

9. THE BRAHMAN AND THE BANKER is a Bengali folktale retold from *Popular Tales of Bengal,* by Kasindranath Banerji (Calcutta: H. D. Chattenjee, 1905).

10. A LAST REQUEST is a Chilean folktale retold from *South American Wonder Tales,* translated and edited by Frances Carpenter (Follett, 1969). Carpenter worked from *Folklore Chilien,* Georgette et Jacques Soustelle, Paris Institut International de Coopération Intellectuelle, 1938. A German variant can be found in *The Complete Grimm's Fairy Tales.*

11. OUTWITTING THE KING is an Ethiopian folktale retold from *The Rich Man and the Singer,* told by Mesfin Habte-Mariam and edited by Christine Price (Dutton, 1971). A Haitian variant can be found in *The Magic Orange Tree,* collected by Diane Wolkstein (Knopf, 1978). The Irish and the Celts also have a tale of hiding in the masses, as told in *Celtic Fairy Tales,* edited by Joseph Jacobs (Nutt, 1982).

12. SUNRISE is a Mexican folktale retold from *Tongues of the Monte,* by J. Frank Dobie (Little, Brown, 1947). Variants can be found in *The Golden Bird: Folk Tales from Slovenia,* by Vladimir Kavčič (World, 1969), and Antti Aarne cites several Scandinavian variants in *The Types of the Folktale* (Burt Franklin, 1971, reprint of 1928 edition).

13. THE TALLEST TALE is a Burmese folktale retold from *Burmese Folk-Tales,* edited by Maung Htin Aung (Oxford University Press, 1948). An Ashanti variant can be found in *The Hat-Shaking Dance,* edited by Harold Courlander (Harcourt, 1957), and a Chinese variant can be found in *Floating Clouds, Floating Dreams,* edited by I. K Dunne (Doubleday, 1974).

14. I first heard the basic tale type of THE BET as a contemporary earthy joke about residents of northern Wisconsin in 1985. My telling is an adaptation and blending of this variant and the equally earthy "Tom and the Master," collected by Roger Abrahams in *The Journal of American Folklore* 83 (1970): 235.

15. THE SHIP is a folk mystery that has intrigued philosophers for centuries. It exists in print as far back as the first century A.D. in Plutarch's *Lives.*